Cover design: Alisha Lofgren

Print ISBN: 978-1-5064-6851-8

Simple Prayers for Children

WRITTEN AND ILLUSTRATED BY HEATHER ELLIS

Augsburg Books
MINNEAPOLIS

Thank you, God, for being my best friend.
You are helpful, loving, and kind,
just like best friends should be.
Our friendship will go on forever.

Amen.

This is fun!
When I try things for the first time,
I will think of you, God.
I will never be scared
because you are right by my side.

Amen.

Even though I can't see you,
I know you are always near
and will never leave me.
Thank you, God, for watching over me.

Amen.

Thank you, God, for making rain.
Thank you for the puddles.
I love jumping in them!

Amen.

I will share my love with others,
just as you shared your love with me.
Thank you, God, for giving us your love.
Thank you that you care.

Amen.

I got stuck up a tree today.
I called for help.
Thank you, God, that you found
a way to sort things out.

Amen.

I tried something new today,
and you were there to help.
I wasn't scared because,
God, you were with me.
Thank you, God, for your patient love.

Amen.

Thank you, God, for thinking of so many
colors for the rainbow.
I love using them in my paintings.
Thank you for color.

Amen.

You are gentle and kind.

You show your wonderful love to all.

I want to be like you.

God, I am glad I can learn from you

every day.

Amen.

Dear God,

When I laugh, I know you laugh with me.
Thank you, God, for making laughter.
Thank you for making me so happy.

Amen.

Thank you, God, for leaves.
I like the crunchy sound they make
when I walk on them.
I love throwing them up into the air!
Thank you, God, for autumn.

Amen.

Father God,
I want to know you always.
I am going to hold on tight
because I never want to let you go.

Amen.

We all look and sound different,
but you love us all.
We speak different languages,
but you understand us, God.
Thank you, God, for loving each one of us.

Amen.

I love singing songs about you, Jesus.

Praising you is what I love best.

Thank you for listening to me.

Amen.

I love flowers.
They are so beautiful.
I love their wonderful perfume and their colors.
Thank you, God, for making flowers.
Thank you, God, for nature.

Amen.

Thank you that I can have fun times
with my friends.
The best friend of all is you, God.
I want to grow closer to you every day.
Thank you for being you.

Amen.

When it comes to sharing,
you give me very good advice.
Thank you, God.

Amen.

Father God,
I like being kind and sharing my things.
Here, you can have the biggest piece!

Amen.

I love birthdays!
Friends come to visit, and we have fun.
There are presents to be opened.
Your love is the best gift of all.
Thank you, God, for birthdays.

Amen.

I want to learn about you, Jesus.
So where can I read about you?
Oh yes, I can find you in Matthew,
Mark, Luke, and John, in my special Bible.

Amen.

I love to pray.
I prayed that you would keep me safe
today, and you did!
Thank you, God, for prayer.
Thank you for keeping me safe.
I promise to pray every day.

Amen.

I love to pray.
Today I felt like praying
in my tent for someone I know!
I am glad that I can pray anywhere.
Thank you, God, for prayer.

Amen.

I love my caregivers.
I love their special cuddles and kisses.
They look after me.
Thank you, God, for my caregivers.

Amen.

When I go to sleep at night,
I know you and your angels are near,
watching over me
and keeping me safe.
Thank you, God, for looking after me.

Amen.

I am amazing!
Thank you, God, for making me special.
You know everything about me.
I am made with your love and care.
I am happy to be me!

Amen.